CONTENTS

Chapter 1 1
Chapter 2 7
Chapter 3 12
Chapter 4 17
Chapter 5 21
Chapter 6 26
Chapter 7 31
Chapter 8 37
Chapter 9 42
Chapter 10 48
Chapter 11 53

CHAPTER 1

When Bianca came to the U.S.
from the Philippines,
everything seemed right.
At last, her life was in order.
She had married
an American GI
who had been stationed
in her country.
Now her husband, Jimmy,
had a good job.
Bianca stayed home
with their baby boy.
Jimmy brought home
good money.
All was well.

Then one day,
Jimmy left.
"I found someone else,"
he told Bianca.

"I want to be with her."
He packed his things.
He and the other woman
moved to another state.
He never asked
to see the child.
He never sent money.
He never even asked Bianca
for a divorce.

So there she was.
Alone, with a baby
and no money.
How could he do this,
she wondered day after day.
But he had.

Bianca couldn't go home.
She didn't have the money.
There was no one here
to move in with.
It never crossed her mind
to go on welfare.
She knew she had to do

what she had seen
other women do.
She must find a job.
A regular paycheck
would pay the rent
and put food on the table.

Luckily for Bianca,
the neighbor upstairs
agreed to watch the baby.
Bianca found a job
at Great Oaks Nursing Home.
She became
a nurse's aide.

The work was hard.
The pay was low.
Bianca didn't speak English well.
But she did love people,
even if they were old or sick.
And the nursing home
paid her health care.
So Bianca was glad
to have this job.

"Good morning, dear,"
she said every day
to every person
in every room.
Some of the people
had things to tell Bianca.
She understood only part
of what they said.
But she smiled
all the while.
The people's faces
would light up
when Bianca came by.

"Here is your breakfast,"
she would say.
She would take a tray
off the food cart.
She would set the tray
in front of the person.

"I think I need
a little help today,"
someone might say.

"I don't feel strong enough
to feed myself."

Bianca understood.
She would spoon the food
into the person's mouth.
She never told anyone
to hurry up.
She just kept on feeding.
She kept on smiling, too.

Thinking It Over

1. If you knew little English,
   what kind of job
   would you be good at?

2. What is Bianca's strong point
   on the job?
   What is her weak point?

3. If you were a person
   in a nursing home,
   would you like Bianca?
   Why or why not?

CHAPTER 2

For the next two years,
Bianca worked at Great Oaks.
Every now and then
she ran into a little problem
because of her English.
But nothing really bad
ever happened because of it.
She got by.
The people loved her
and she loved them.
That seemed to be
all that mattered.

Then one day
something did go wrong.

Every morning,
Bianca took the food trays
to the rooms.
Then she would come back
to feed Mr. Bender.

She fed him every day.
It was part of her rounds.

On this day
there was a new sign
over Mr. Bender's bed.
It read,
"NOTHING BY MOUTH."
The sign was there
because Mr. Bender
was seeing Dr. Cook today.
The doctor had said
Mr. Bender could have
no food in him this morning.
But Bianca wasn't sure
what the sign said.
And Mr. Bender
didn't know it was there,
or he might have told her.

"Here is your breakfast,"
said Bianca.
She set the tray
in front of Mr. Bender.

Handle with Care

She began to feed him.
When he finished,
she took the tray and left.

A few hours later,
Mr. Bender was wheeled out
to a treatment room.
"Did you have
anything to eat this morning?"
asked Dr. Cook.

"I don't remember eating,"
said the old man.
He forgot all about Bianca
feeding him breakfast.
So Dr. Cook
gave Mr. Bender the treatment.
Then he was wheeled
back to his room.

At lunch time,
Bianca came in
to feed Mr. Bender.
He seemed to be sleeping.

"Wake up, Mr. Bender!"
said Bianca.

He did not wake up.
Bianca shook him a little bit.
"Time for lunch!"
she said.
He still did not wake up.

Bianca felt his head.
He was warm.
She felt under his nose.
A little warm air
was coming out.
But the man did not wake up.

Now Bianca was afraid.
She looked up
to find the button
to call Nurse Jackson.
She saw the sign again—
"NOTHING BY MOUTH."
"I wonder
what that sign says,"
she said to herself.

Thinking It Over

1. Do you think
   a nurse's aide
   should have to pass
   an English test
   before starting the job?

2. Think of a job
   you know about.
   When would a person
   have to use reading and math
   on this job?

3. Think of this same job.
   What could go wrong
   if the person on this job
   has trouble
   with reading and math?

CHAPTER 3

In a matter of seconds,
Nurse Jackson and Dr. Cook
were at Mr. Bender's side.
The nurse gave him CPR.
At first, nothing happened.
Mr. Bender still didn't wake up.
But after a few more tries,
he began to open his eyes.

Nurse Jackson called
for someone to wheel Mr. Bender
down to the hospital wing.

"How did this happen?"
Dr. Cook asked.
"The man was fine
when I gave him the treatment
this morning.
He told me
he didn't eat breakfast.

But if he did eat something,
that is why he passed out."

"I fed him breakfast,"
said Bianca.

"You did?"
said the doctor.
He seemed very worried.
"Can't you read the sign?
It says,
'NOTHING BY MOUTH.' "

"I'm so sorry,"
said Bianca.
"I don't read
English so good!"
She began to cry.

Dr. Cook turned
to Nurse Jackson.
"Did you know
this aide cannot read?"
he asked her.
"You should have told Bianca

Mr. Bender was not supposed
to eat anything this morning."

"Bianca has worked here
for two years,"
said the nurse.
"Her English isn't very strong.
And the progress notes
she writes on people
are a bit weak.
But I never had reason
to believe she couldn't read."

"That man could have died,"
said the doctor.
"You are very lucky.
If he had died,
you could have lost your license."

"I'm not the one
who fed Mr. Bender,"
said the nurse.

"That doesn't matter,"
said the doctor.

Handle with Care   **15**

"Slip-ups by your aides
are *your* slip-ups.
You're the one
who gets into trouble
if they do something wrong.
You must keep on top
of everything your aides do."

"Yes, Dr. Cook,"
said Nurse Jackson.
"And you, Bianca,
must keep an eye out
for new signs.
If you can't read them,
ask me about them.
Do you understand?"

Bianca said she did.
But all she understood
was "new signs."
She did know
that from now on
she should watch out
for new signs.

Thinking It Over

1. Suppose you are
   a person who cannot read.
   What kinds of things
   might you *not* see?

2. How would you feel
   if something bad happened
   because of you?

3. How do you think
   people who cannot read
   get by without others knowing?

CHAPTER 4

"Well, now I know
you can't read,"
said Nurse Jackson
to Bianca one day.
"Can you add and subtract?"

"Yes, a little,"
said Bianca.

"Then I want to show you
how to find out
if a person is not passing
enough water,"
said Nurse Jackson.
"First, you write down
the weight of all the food
the person eats.
Then you write down
how much water
has passed into this bag."

"I can do that,"
said Bianca.

"I need a record
on these four people,"
said Nurse Jackson.
She pointed out their names
on a sheet of paper.
"I'll show you
where their rooms are."

Bianca enjoyed keeping track
of how much went in and out
of the four people.
She checked every weight twice
before she wrote down
the numbers.
Then she gave the paper
to Nurse Jackson.

"The numbers look good,"
said Nurse Jackson.
"All these people
are passing enough water.
Thanks for a good job."

Bianca felt as if
she knew what she was doing.
Then one morning,
she was in a hurry.
She didn't check her numbers.
She just wrote them down.
She gave the paper
to Nurse Jackson,
just like always.

"Numbers look fine,"
said Nurse Jackson,
just like always.

But Mrs. O'Day's numbers
were not fine.
Bianca had not subtracted right.
It looked as if
Mrs. O'Day was passing
enough water.
But she was not.
The woman
was in trouble
and no one knew it.

Thinking It Over

1. Why is it important
   to keep track
   of certain numbers?

2. What can happen
   if you try to do something
   too fast?
   How much time
   does it take to be careful?

CHAPTER 5

That afternoon
Bianca again checked
Mrs. O'Day's numbers.
That's when she saw
that the water in the bag
was much too low.

Bianca told Nurse Jackson
right away.
The nurse was able
to help Mrs. O'Day.

Thank heaven,
Bianca said to herself.
Mrs. O'Day would be OK.
No one would have to know
about the wrong number.

But Bianca's troubles
with math and reading
were not over.

That same afternoon
she walked right into a room
with a sign on the door.
It said,
"DO NOT ENTER
UNLESS WEARING
GOWN AND GLOVES."
Bianca walked right by it.

She needed to pick up
dirty clothes and sheets.
Only one person was in the room.
She pulled the sheets off his bed.
She put on clean sheets.
She stuffed the old sheets
into the big laundry bag.
Then she headed downstairs
to the laundry room.

"Here is everything
from wing 2D,"
she said.

"Where's the red 'I' bag?"
asked the laundry woman.

"What 'I'* bag?"
asked Bianca.

"There's a man with AIDS
in wing 2D,"
said the laundry woman.
"His things should be
in a special 'I' bag.
Didn't you see
the sign on his door?"

"Oh, no!"
cried Bianca.
She began to cry again.
"Oh, I'm so stupid!
I can't read the signs!
I touched the sheets
of someone with AIDS!
My hands were not covered!

---

* The "I" stands for *isolation*—kept apart
from everything else. Laundry for
patients carrying infectious diseases
(AIDS, hepatitis, etc.) must be placed
in one of these special bags. The person
who handles the laundry must be
properly protected with gloves, a
coverall gown, and perhaps a mask.

I wasn't wearing a gown!
Now I'll get AIDS, too!
I'm going to die!"

"Call the AIDS number,"
said the laundry woman.
"You can find out
how to get an AIDS test."

"I will, I will,"
cried Bianca.
"Oh, please don't tell anyone
I did this.
They'll fire me.
I need this job
to feed my little boy!
Oh, please don't tell!"

"I won't tell anyone,"
said the laundry woman.
"I'll put your whole bag
in the very hot wash.
But you better call that number.
And don't you touch me, lady!
I don't want to die, too!"

Thinking It Over

1. What do you know about AIDS?

2. Do you think Bianca will get AIDS? Why or why not?

3. What should people do if they think they have AIDS?

CHAPTER 6

When Bianca got home,
she grabbed the phone book.
She looked under AIDS.
There was nothing there.
She was sure
the laundry woman had said
there was an AIDS number.
But she couldn't find it
in the white pages.

Then she remembered
the special pages
for numbers of human services.
Sure enough,
Bianca found "AIDS Hotline"
in those pages.
She pushed the buttons
on her phone.

"Hello," she said.
"I don't speak English
so very good.
I think I got AIDS today.
I did not see the sign."
She told the man
about touching the sheets.

"Did you handle
any needles
from this person?"
asked the man.

"No," said Bianca.
"I'm not a nurse,
just an aide."

"Now try not to worry,"
said the man's voice.
"You did not touch
the person's blood.
And you had no open cuts.
You probably did not get AIDS."

"Can someone test me?"
Bianca asked.
"I must know for sure."

"It's much too soon,"
the man explained.
"An AIDS test won't tell anything
in less than six weeks.
It might not tell anything
for six months or more."

"I would feel better
if I knew for sure,"
said Bianca.

"Why don't you wait
a few more months?"
said the man.
"Then you can go
to the state health center.
They will be happy
to give you a free AIDS test.
But, really, Miss,
it would be a big surprise
if you had AIDS."

The man was trying
to help Bianca feel better.
But she was still shook up.
She wondered
how she could wait for months
to know for sure.

She picked up her son
and held him tight.
Then she put him
in her bed
and fell asleep beside him.

Thinking It Over

1. What is the best way
   to talk to someone
   as shook up as Bianca?

2. Have you ever
   had to wait a long time
   to find out about your health?
   How did it feel?

3. Is there a special page
   in your phone book
   with numbers
   of human services?
   What numbers on those pages
   might you need sometime?

CHAPTER 7

The next day at work
Bianca didn't talk
about what had happened.
She didn't want anyone
to think she had AIDS.
She was afraid
that no one would want
to be near her.

Many of the other nurse's aides
had something else
on their minds.
They were talking
about a different kind of test.
If they passed the test,
they would be certified
as nurse's aides.
They were going
to a special class.
There they learned

what they needed to know
to pass the test.

Bianca did not need
to take the test.
She had worked
at Great Oaks
for more than two years.
A nurse's aide
who had worked
in one nursing home
for over two years
didn't need to take the test.

In a way,
Bianca was glad.
She felt she knew
how to take care of people.
And it would be very hard
to get ready
for the test.

In another way,
she wished she did

have to take the test.
She felt left out.
Everyone was talking
about the class and the test.
She had nothing to say.
She also wondered
if she might learn things.
Maybe she wouldn't be
in trouble now
if she had taken that class.

"You're lucky,"
said Dody Silva.
"You get to go home
right after work.
There's nothing
I'd like more, kid.
We have to stay here
and hit the books."

Bianca just smiled.
"What did you learn
in yesterday's class?"
she asked.

"How to feed someone
so they don't choke,"
said another aide.
"Now, isn't that something?"

"I know how to do that.
Just ask Mr. Bender,"
Bianca said.
"What else did you learn?"
she asked.

"How to read and write,"
laughed Dody.
"We learned
how to write
better progress notes.
One day we even learned
how to talk to people.
Like how to be nice
and stuff like that."

"Sometimes that's hard,"
said Bianca.

"You're always nice,"
said Dody.
"Sometimes I don't have
the time of day
for the cranky old ladies."

"Tell me what else
you learn in that class,"
begged Bianca.

"How to handle
people in 'I' rooms,"
said Dody.

Bianca said nothing.
The subject of "I" rooms
gave her too much pain.
She wished
with all her heart
that she could have read
that sign yesterday.

Thinking It Over

1. What are some reasons people on the job might take a class?

2. Would you ever want to take a class that you didn't have to?

3. Do you think workers such as nurse's aides might be better if they had to study for a test?

CHAPTER 8

At lunch time,
Bianca headed for the kitchen
to get her food cart.
On her way down the hall,
she heard loud voices
coming from one room.
She walked up
to hear what was going on.

It was Dody Silva.
She was yelling
at Mrs. Hatfield
in the first bed.
"I told you to sit up!"
shouted Dody.
"I mean now!
I don't have all day
to feed old bags like you."

"I can't sit up,"
cried Mrs. Hatfield.

"I'm not strong enough.
I need help."

"I help you enough!"
shouted Dody.
She grabbed Mrs. Hatfield
by the arm.
She shook her.
The food tray
spilled all over her.

"Look what you've done!"
cried Mrs. Hatfield.

"I don't need
any back talk, either!"
Dody shouted.

Bianca ran
into the room.
"Take it easy,"
she told Dody.
"Why don't you step out?
I'll take care
of Mrs. Hatfield."

Dody left the room.
Bianca cleaned up Mrs. Hatfield.
Then she got the woman
a new food tray.
She helped her sit up.
She fed her
as if she were a baby.

"Thank you
for being so kind,"
said Mrs. Hatfield.

When Bianca finished
feeding Mrs. Hatfield,
she went to look for Dody.

"That was pretty mean talk,"
Bianca told Dody.
"Sometimes I get angry
with the old people, too.
You know what I do?
I give a little smile.
Then I say,
'I'll be back.'
I walk out of the room.

I count to 10.
Then I go back in
with a clear head.
It really works."

"I'll try it next time,"
said Dody.
"But I'm not sweet like you.
I fly off the handle
with no trouble at all!"

"You can work
on being nice,"
said Bianca.
"What if you were the one
in that bed?
Think how you would feel.
You wouldn't want someone
to scream at you."

"I guess not,"
said Dody.
"Thanks, kid.
I'm going to take a break.
Then I'll get back to work."

Thinking It Over

1. How do you deal with old or sick people?

2. What does a person like Bianca have that she didn't learn from a book?

3. What is something you know that you didn't learn in school or from a book?

CHAPTER 9

Later the same day,
Bianca was going around
to write progress notes
on her people.
She didn't like this job.
She had to ask the people
how they felt.
She had to ask them
what words to use.
She even had to ask them
how to spell the words
so she could write them.
Nurse Jackson
had never said anything
against Bianca's progress notes.
Bianca could only hope
she didn't write something
that would hurt someone.

She stopped by
to see Mrs. Hatfield.
"How are you this afternoon?"
Bianca asked.

Mrs. Hatfield
was having trouble talking.
"I — can't — seem—
to — get — enough — air,"
said Mrs. Hatfield.
She had to stop
between each word
to catch her breath.

"I'll write it down,"
said Bianca.
It was clear
that Mrs. Hatfield
couldn't help spell the words.
"Trouble to catch breath,"
she wrote on the progress notes.
"You'll be OK soon,"
she told Mrs. Hatfield.

"You're probably still upset
about what happened at lunch."

Bianca went on
to the other rooms.
She didn't think much
about Mrs. Hatfield.
She had seen many people
have trouble catching their breath.
It had always been
because they were upset.
It always went away
in a little while.

When she finished
all her progress notes,
she gave them
to Nurse Jackson.

"What's this one?"
asked the nurse.
"'Trouble to catch breath.'
What do you mean?"

"Mrs. Hatfield
takes a deep breath
between every word,"
Bianca explained.
"I've seen it before."

"Have you ever seen this
with Mrs. Hatfield?"
Nurse Jackson asked.

"Well, no,"
said Bianca.

Nurse Jackson's face
turned to stone.
"Come with me!"
she called,
as she ran
toward Mrs. Hatfield's room.

"We must all use
the same clear words,"
said Nurse Jackson as she ran.

"All the nurse's aides
studying for the test
are learning these words.
To say only
'Trouble to catch breath'
is not clear enough.
What's more,
you should have told me
what was happening right away.
Mrs. Hatfield
might be in big trouble."

By the time
they got to her,
Mrs. Hatfield looked blue.
She waved her arms
in the air.
She could not seem
to get any air at all.
Then she passed out.

Thinking It Over

1. Why can it be important
   to use the right words
   when telling about some
   things?

2. Are there ever times
   in your life
   when you see something
   you need to learn more about?

3. Sometimes you can
   do things
   in the same old way
   you've always done them.
   Why doesn't that always work?

CHAPTER 10

The doctors
tried to bring Mrs. Hatfield
back to life.
But they couldn't.
She was gone.
They explained
that something was wrong
inside her lungs.
It probably had nothing to do
with being upset
at lunch time.

Bianca felt very bad.
She had felt so lucky
when Mr. Bender was OK.
"If only I knew
the right words,"
she cried.
"Maybe we could have saved
poor Mrs. Hatfield."

Handle with Care 49

"You feel bad,"
said Nurse Jackson.
"But I feel worse.
I'm sorry
that Mrs. Hatfield is dead.
But my neck is on the line."

"You?" asked Bianca.
"I'm the one
who wrote down
the wrong words."

"I'm the R.N. over you,"
said Nurse Jackson.
"Everything falls on me.
They could take away
my license for this."

"Oh, no!"
sobbed Bianca.
"That's not fair."

"That's the law,"
said Nurse Jackson.
"I am sure

that this will come up
before the board.
We'll just have to wait
and see what happens."

"So much to wait for!"
cried Bianca.
"I also must wait
to see if I have AIDS."
She told Nurse Jackson
about missing the sign
on the "I" room door.

"I really believe
you will test out fine,"
said Nurse Jackson.
"You did not touch any blood.
You did not touch anything
from the person's body.
And you had no open cuts."

"No matter what happens,
I have made up my mind
about something,"
said Bianca.

"What's that?"
Nurse Jackson asked.

"I will take that class,"
said Bianca.
"I will take that test
to get certified.
There are things
I need to learn
to be a really good nurse's aide.
I can't keep making
these bad slip-ups."

"You have worked here
for over two years,"
said Nurse Jackson.
"You do not need
to take the test."

"That is not the point,"
said Bianca.
"I must become better.
To pass the test
is the only way."

Thinking It Over

1. If you were on the board, would you take away Nurse Jackson's license?

2. If you were Bianca, would you take the test, even if you didn't have to?

CHAPTER 11

Many things happened
in the next few months.
The matter of Mrs. Hatfield
did come before the board.
Nurse Jackson and Bianca
both had to speak
at a hearing.
The board members
listened to the story.
They asked many questions.

The board decided
not to take away
Nurse Jackson's license.
Their reason was
that Bianca wrote down
what she saw.
Nurse Jackson
saw the progress notes

as soon as possible.
She did everything she could
as fast as she could.
During the same month,
Bianca had a blood test for AIDS.
She was told
that she did not have AIDS.
If she still wasn't sure,
she could take the test again
after a few more months.
She decided not to.
She felt safe
after the first test.

All this time,
Bianca had been going
to the class for nurse's aides.
She had worked hard.
Every night
after her son went to sleep,
Bianca studied for the test.
She learned the English words
for many things
she already knew.
She went over everything

Handle with Care

with her friends at work.
Then the time came
to take the test.

In a few weeks
she heard the news.
She had passed the test.
So had Dody Silva
and the others.
What a great day!
That night,
the aides who weren't working
went out to dinner together.
Bianca couldn't remember
the last time
she had felt so happy.

But the real test would be
whether Bianca
would become
a better nurse's aide.
There would be
many such tests.
The first real test
came the very next day.

Mr. Bender
had been having trouble
with his blood sugar.
The doctor put up
a new sign
above Mr. Bender's bed.
He was not supposed
to eat candy or ice cream.
He missed sugar very much.
He had had a sweet tooth
all his life.

Bianca wheeled
the food cart
to Mr. Bender's door.
She lifted off his tray.
The kitchen already knew
not to give him sweets.
Bianca didn't know yet.

Then she spotted
the new sign
above Mr. Bender's bed.
"DIABETIC,"
it read.

Bianca knew right away
what that meant.
It meant no sweets
for Mr. Bender.

"That was a fine lunch,"
said Mr. Bender
when he finished eating.
"The ham was great!
I even liked the beans.
But where is my cake?
I'll tell you what.
I'll give you a dollar.
You run out and buy me
some real ice cream.
Would you do that for me?"

Bianca pointed
to the sign.
"I can read, Mr. Bender,"
she said.
"You are diabetic.
No ice cream for you.
Sorry.
An order is an order."

"Please, just this once?"
Mr. Bender begged.

"Just this once
could kill you,"
said Bianca.
"Now, I'm a certified nurse's aide.
So I know this.
Besides, I like you too much
to give you sugar."

Bianca reached over
and took Mr. Bender's hand.
"I want you around
for a long time."

The old man
smiled at Bianca.
"You're good.
You're really good.
You not only know your job.
You're a friend, too.
I can live without sugar.
But I can't live
without you."

Handle with Care

That made Bianca's day.
Now she knew for sure
her reason for being here.
She had always had
lots of love to give.
Now she had the know-how
to back it up.
And she was doing it all
in English!

"Now take a little rest,"
she told Mr. Bender.
"I'll check in with you
before I go home."

She turned out the light.
She closed the door.
Then she went
to help someone else.

Thinking It Over

1. Why is it important
   to not give in
   when someone
   asks for something
   that could bring trouble?

2. What are the things
   that make you feel
   you are doing a good job?

3. What makes
   a worker like Bianca
   so special?